EMB

Variations

Connie Westenberg

FORTE PUBLISHERS

Contents

Fourth printing May 2004
ISBN 90 5877 362 0

This is a publication from
Forte Publishers BV
P.O. Box 1394
3500 BJ Utrecht
The Netherlands

For more information about the creative books available from Forte Uitgevers:
www.hobby-party.com

Publisher: Els Neele
Editor: Hanny Vlaar
Photography: Marc Wouters
Styling: Connie Westenberg
Cover and inner design:
BADE creatieve communicatie,
Baarn, the Netherlands

Preface

When I was asked, some time ago, to write a **CraftSpecial** book using the latest

Fiskars products, the answer was obvious. Which crafter would not want to use

these excellent materials? The inspiration for the many different cards soon

followed. Once you get started, it is often difficult to stop, because there are so

many variations and combinations when embossing. The latest Fiskars embossing

products, such as the Texture plates, the Mini ShapeBoss, the ShapeBoss and

the CardBoss, provide many options for making greetings cards. With this book,

I have tried to pass on as many ideas as possible with a varied use of materials, such

as vellum, metal foil and different types of paper. I know you will be as enthusiastic as I am about

the many variations with embossing.

Connie

Good luck.

Techniques

1. The ShapeBoss stencil set

For this set you need special transparent and grey embossing stencils and a dual-tip stylus with a large and a small tip. This method of embossing does not require a light box and it is, therefore, also possible to emboss dark coloured card. It is also possible to emboss thin paper, such as vellum and embossing foil. The set consists of a blue tray, which has holes around the border in which orange pegs are inserted, and a grey and a transparent stencil set made from flexible plastic (24 x 31 cm). The stencils have the same embossing pattern. First, place the grey stencil on the tray. Next, place the transparent stencil on top and secure both stencils by placing orange pegs in opposite corners (for texts, place the stencils as a mirror image to the desired result). Place the card in the correct position between both stencils and use more pegs to prevent it from sliding about. The centimetre scale on the transparent stencil helps to keep the card straight. Use the large tip of the stylus to copy the pattern onto the card. Follow the contours of the pattern and carefully push the card into the openings in the bottom stencil. Follow the lines once or twice more using the small tip, pushing slightly harder. If you also wish to emboss another part of the card, you can move the card or use the pegs to secure the stencils in a different place.

Tip

Rub the area that is going to be embossed with a candle. This will make the stylus glide more easily over the paper. You can also rub the tip of the stylus over the candle so that you do not get a layer of wax on the card.

2. The Mini ShapeBoss stencil set

For this set you need special transparent and grey stencils and a dual-tip stylus with a large and a small tip (a smaller stylus than the stylus in the ShapeBoss set). The Mini ShapeBoss also has a storage space, where materials can be kept. Since a light source is not necessary using the Mini ShapeBoss, you can take it with you when you go away or you can use it in the garden. The grey and transparent Mini ShapeBoss stencils can also be used on the CardBoss.

3. The CardBoss stencil set

For this set you need special transparent and orange embossing stencils and a dual-tip stylus with a large and a small tip. The patterns on these stencils are the same size as an A6 card.

1. The ShapeBoss stencil set

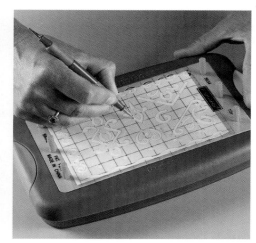

2. The Mini ShapeBoss stencil set

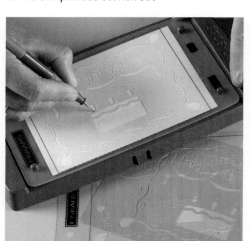

3. The CardBoss stencil set

4. Texture plates

4. Texture plates (templates for embossing backgrounds)

Each pack contains two strong, blue templates which have a different pattern on either side. Use the orange pegs to secure the templates to a Fiskars ShapeBoss or Mini ShapeBoss tray or just place them on a table. You can emboss both card and paper (100 gram) using the Texture plates. It is recommended to use paper if you are not very strong. Secure the card to be embossed to the template using non-permanent adhesive tape (for example, napkin tape). Rub the part of the paper or card to be embossed with a candle so that the tip of the stylus glides easily over the paper or card. Firmly run the larger tip of the stylus over the card or paper (the large tip of the stylus from the ShapeBoss set works best and is available separately). The patterns will be slightly visible. Push harder until you can clearly see the patterns. Next, use the small tip of the stylus (for example, the stylus from the Mini ShapeBoss set or CardBoss set, which are also available separately) and push the contours of the pattern into the card. Push the lines firmly into the card several times.

Victorian Mini ShapeBoss stencil

Materials

- Card (220 gram): Artoz and Canson Mi-Teintes
- Artoz paper (100 gram)
- Vellum: mother-of-pearl, blue and green
- CardBoss stencils (Kars)
- Picture Punch sheets (Vaessen)
- Bison spray glue

- Amaco embossing foil: gold and silver
- Photo glue, double-sided adhesive tape
- Cutting mat and cutting knife
- Transparent ruler with a metal cutting edge
- Pencil and eraser

- Candle
- 3D glue/foam tape
- Fiskars products:
- ShapeBoss stencil set
- Mini ShapeBoss stencil set
- CardBoss stencil set
- Texture plates
- Stylus (large and small tips)
- Border punches

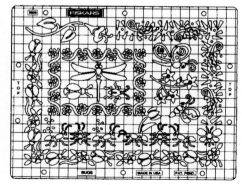

Critters ShapeBoss stencil

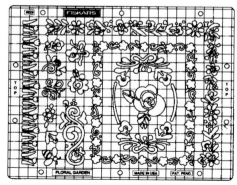

Floral Garden ShapeBoss stencil

Insects

A nice combination of embossed borders and backgrounds.

What you need
- ❏ *Artoz card: fawn (241)*
- ❏ *Canson Mi-Teintes card: apple green (475), almond green (480), earth red (130), pink (481) and dark pink (352)*
- ❏ *ShapeBoss stencil set*
- ❏ *Texture plates*
- ❏ *Stylus (small tip)*
- ❏ *Candle*
- ❏ *3D glue*

General information
All the cards measure 14.5 x 14.5 cm.
A large fawn square (14 x 14 cm) upon which a frame is embossed is stuck on every card. The small fawn square is stuck to the card using 3D glue or foam tape.

Embossing the frame
Since the top stencil is transparent, you can easily determine where the patterns can be embossed.

Making backgrounds with the Texture plates
Emboss the backgrounds with one of the patterns on the Texture plates (see Techniques). You do not have to emboss the area where you will stick another piece of card.

1. Dragonfly
Double apple green card • ShapeBoss embossing stencil – Critters • Texture plate – Energy (dots)
Embossing the frame: the long side of the pattern fits exactly onto the sides of the frame. Emboss two patterns with a double streamer between them at the top and bottom. Draw a square (6.3 x 6.3 cm) on a piece of fawn card. Emboss the dragonfly, making sure most of it is within the square. Cut the square out along the pencil lines, paying attention to the wings. Stick the square on an almond green square (6.8 x 6.8 cm). Cut an apple green square (9.5 x 9.5 cm) and emboss the dots from the Texture plate on it. Stick all the parts together as shown in the photograph.

2. Beetles
Double apple green card • ShapeBoss embossing stencil – Critters • Texture plate – Energy (bubbles)

Embossing the frame: four patterns which are next to each other on the stencil fit exactly along the right-hand side. Start in the bottom right-hand corner and emboss a beetle, a flower, a beetle and then another flower. Continue embossing the pattern around the card, moving the card to emboss each side. Emboss alternate beetles and flowers. Draw a square (4.3 x 4.3 cm) on a piece of fawn card. Emboss a beetle and some leaves in the square. Also emboss two dots on the beetle's shell. Cut the square out along the lines, paying attention to the antenna. Stick the square at an angle on an apple green square (6 x 6 cm). Cut an almond green square (8.7 x 8.7 cm) and emboss the background of bubbles on it. Stick all the parts together as shown in the photograph.

3. Tulips

Double earth red card • ShapeBoss embossing stencil – Floral garden • Texture plate – Nature (leaves)

Embossing the frame: start by embossing a small tulip in every corner. Next, emboss a large tulip in the middle of each side. If you move the card, you will see that you can emboss another two small tulips on both sides. Draw a square (4.5 x 4.5 cm) on a piece of fawn card.

Place the square on the ShapeBoss tray with one point of the square facing downwards and emboss a couple of tulips and a bee on it. Cut the square out along the pencil lines, paying attention to the wing. Stick the square on an earth red square (6.3 x 6.3 cm). Cut a dark pink square (8.5 x 8.5 cm) and emboss leaf patterns from the Texture plate on each side. Stick all the parts together as shown in the photograph.

4. Rose

Double earth red card • ShapeBoss embossing stencil – Floral garden • Texture plate – Energy (fabric)

Embossing the frame: place one of the sides of the embossing pattern along the top of the card. Move the card back and forth until there is a corner pattern in both corners and emboss the pattern. Turn the card around and emboss patterns along the other sides, making sure they look continuous as much as possible. Cut an earth red square (10 x 10 cm) and emboss a background using the fabric pattern. Draw a square (6 x 6 cm) on a piece of fawn card and emboss a rose on it. Cut the square out along the pencil lines, paying attention to the leaves, and stick it on a pink square (6.5 x 6.5 cm).

Autumn leaves

Once the wind starts to blow, the trees loose their attractively coloured leaves.

What you need
- ❏ *Canson Mi-Teintes card: almond green (480), salmon (384) and maize (470)*
- ❏ *Brown paper*
- ❏ *Shake-it cutting sheet (IT 322)*
- ❏ *Texture plates*
- ❏ *Stylus: large and small tip*
- ❏ *Candle*
- ❏ *3D glue*

Cutting diamond shapes
Draw a rectangle and use a pencil to draw a dot in the middle of each side. Cut the corners off.

Cutting a square in four
Draw diagonal lines on a square and cut along the lines.

1. Large diamond
Texture plate – Energy (bubbles)
Make a maize double card (14.8 x 10.5 cm) and a brown rectangle (13 x 9.5 cm). Cut a diamond from a brown rectangle (11 x 7.5 cm) and another one from a salmon rectangle (10 x 6 cm). Emboss the background in the corners of the salmon diamond and cut the corners off. Place the brown diamond on the back of a green rectangle (12.8 x 8.5 cm). Use a pencil to indicate where the diamond will be stuck and mark 0.5 cm around the four sides of the brown diamond. Emboss the corners of the green rectangle. Cut a maize rectangle (5 x 3 cm) and emboss the background on it. Stick all the parts together as shown in the photograph. Use glue to stick the green leaf on the card and use 3D glue or foam tape to stick the autumn leaf on the green leaf.

2. Chestnut
Texture plate – Energy (fabric)
Make a green double card (14 x 14 cm) and a brown square (13 x 13 cm). Cut a brown square (7.5 x 7.5 cm) and place it on the back of a salmon square (12 x 12 cm). Use a pencil to indicate where the brown square will be stuck at an angle. Emboss the corners of the salmon square, remaining 0.5 cm from the pencil lines. Cut a green square (5.6 x 5.6 cm) and a maize square (5 x 5 cm) and emboss the background on them. Cut the green square in four and stick

all the parts together as shown in the photograph. Make the chestnut leaf 3D.

3. Acorns
Texture plate – Nature (wood grain)
Make a salmon double card (14 x 14 cm) and a brown square (13 x 13 cm). Cut a brown square (6.5 x 6.5 cm) and place it on the back of a green square (12 x 12 cm). Use a pencil to indicate where the brown square will be stuck. Emboss the frame on the green square, remaining 0.5 cm from the pencil lines. Cut a salmon square (4 x 4 cm) and a maize square (4.5 x 4.5 cm) and emboss the background on them. Cut the salmon square in four and stick the parts together as shown in the photograph. Make the leaves and acorns 3D.

4. Small diamond
Texture plate – Nature (stone)
Make a green double card (14.8 x 10.5 cm) and a brown rectangle (13.8 x 9.5 cm). Cut a brown rectangle (9 x 4.5 cm) and place it on the back of a maize rectangle (12.8 x 8.5 cm). Use a pencil to indicate where the brown rectangle will be stuck. Emboss a frame on the maize rectangle, remaining 0.5 cm from the pencil lines. Cut two salmon rectangles (4.3 x 2 cm) and emboss the background on them. Cut the rectangles diagonally through the middle. Cut a green diamond from a rectangle (7 x 3.5 cm) and emboss the background on it. Stick all the parts together as shown in the photograph. Make the leaves and acorn 3D.

Pumpkins

Attractive cards with

pumpkins in different

colours and sizes.

What you need
- ❏ *Artoz card: honey yellow (243), birch green (305), azure (393) and lobster red (545)*
- ❏ *Pumpkin cutting sheet (Anke Nobel)*
- ❏ *Texture plates*
- ❏ *Stylus: large and small tip*
- ❏ *Candle*
- ❏ *3D glue*

1. Butterflies
Texture plate – Energy (fabric)
Make a honey yellow double card (14.8 x 10.5 cm) and a birch green rectangle (13.8 x 9.5 cm). Cut all the parts of the rectangular picture separately out of the cutting sheet. Turn the birch green card over. Place the pumpkins in the corners and place the blue frame on the card as shown in the photograph. Use a pencil to indicate where these will be stuck on the card. Remove the pictures and emboss the background in the corners in the two triangles which will be visible next to the pumpkins. Cut an azure rectangle (5 x 4.5 cm) and emboss the same background on it. Stick all the parts together as shown in the photograph. Stick the picture from the cutting sheet in the middle and make it 3D using separate pictures from the cutting sheet.

2. Pumpkin leaves
Texture plate – Energy (bubbles)
Make a lobster red double card (14 x 14 cm). Cut two birch green squares (10 x 10 cm and 5 x 5 cm) and a honey yellow square (5 x 5 cm). Emboss the background on the three squares and cut them diagonally in four. Cut a honey yellow square (11 x 11 cm). Cut all the parts of the square picture separately out of the cutting sheet. Place the pieces you wish to use for your card on the back of the large honey yellow square. Use a pencil to indicate the square within which the large pumpkin and the four surrounding blue corners will be located. Next, emboss the background only in the places which will not be covered by a picture, i.e. all the sides next to the large pumpkin. Turn the honey yellow card over and stick all the parts on the double card as shown in the picture.

Stick the pumpkin leaves in the corners using 3D glue as shown in the photograph. Make the picture in the middle 3D using separate pictures from the cutting sheet.

3. Pumpkin leaves
Texture plate – Nature (wood grain)
For this card, use the parts of the cutting sheet which were not used for card 2. Make an azure double card (14 x 14 cm). Cut a honey yellow square (13 x 13 cm) and a birch green square (8 x 8 cm). Turn the honey yellow card over and indicate where the frame of pumpkin leaves and the green square will be located. Emboss the background on the remaining area. Do the same with the green square. Turn the square over and indicate where the middle picture and the corner pictures will be located. Emboss the remaining area. Stick all the parts together as shown in the photograph. Make the picture in the middle 3D using separate pictures from the cutting sheet.

4. Garden scene
Texture plate – Energy (squares)
For this card, use the parts of the cutting sheet which were not used for card 1. Make a birch green double card (14.8 x 10.5 cm) and a honey yellow rectangle (13.8 x 9.5 cm). Turn the honey yellow card over and use a pencil to indicate where all the triangles will be stuck on the card. Emboss the background only in the squares in the corners. Cut an azure square (7 x 7 cm) and emboss the background on it. Turn the embossed cards over and stick all the parts on the card as shown in the picture. Stick the pumpkins in the corners using 3D glue. Make the picture in the middle 3D using separate pictures from the cutting sheet.

It's autumn

It's time to put your boots

on, because the rain is

coming.

What you need
- ❏ Card: lilac (Artoz 453), light green, moss green, light blue and mustard yellow
- ❏ Autumn cutting sheet (Anke Nobel)
- ❏ Texture plates
- ❏ Stylus: large and small tip
- ❏ Candle
- ❏ 3D glue

1. Autumn leaves
Texture plate – Energy (fabric)
Make a dark green double card (14.8 x 10.5 cm) and a light green rectangle (13.8 x 9.5 cm). Cut all the parts of the rectangular picture separately out of the cutting sheet. Place the parts you wish to use for your card on the back of the light green rectangle. Use a pencil to indicate where the squares will be located in the corners and the diagonal lines above them. Emboss the background only on the two light green triangles. Cut a mustard yellow square and emboss the background on it. Stick all the parts together as shown in the photograph. Stick the picture from the cutting sheet in the middle. Make the pictures 3D using separate pictures from the cutting sheet.

2. It's time to put your boots on
Texture plate – Nature (wood grain)
Make a mustard yellow double card (14 x 14 cm) and a light green square (13 x 13 cm). Cut all the parts of the square picture separately out of the

cutting sheet. Place the pieces you wish to use for your card on the back of the light green square. Use a pencil to indicate the square in which the autumn picture and the four surrounding triangles will be located. Also indicate where the pink frame will be located. Next, emboss the background only on the remaining area. Cut a moss green square (5.2 x 5.2 cm) and emboss the background only in the corners. Stick all the parts together as shown in the photograph. Make the picture in the middle 3D using the separate pictures from the cutting sheet.

3. Autumn storm
Texture plate – Energy (dots)

For this card, use the parts of the cutting sheet which were not used for card 2. Make a lilac double card (14 x 14 cm). Cut a mustard yellow square (10 x 10 cm) and emboss the background on it. Cut the square diagonally in four. Cut a light green square (11 x 11 cm). Cut a light blue square (4.8 x 4.8 cm) and emboss the background on it. Stick the picture on it and cut the corners at an angle. Stick all the parts together as shown in the photograph. Make the picture in the middle 3D using separate pictures from the cutting sheet.

4. Birds
Texture plate – Energy (dots)

For this card, use the parts of the cutting sheet which were not used for card 1. Make a light green double card (14.8 x 10.5 cm) and a moss green rectangle (13.8 x 9.5 cm). Cut all the parts of the rectangular picture separately out of the cutting sheet. Cut four mustard yellow squares (2.3 x 2.3 cm) and emboss the background on them. Cut a light blue square (6.5 x 6.5 cm) and emboss the background on it. Stick all the parts together as shown in the photograph. Stick the picture from the cutting sheet in the middle. Make the pictures 3D using separate pictures from the cutting sheet. Stick the leaves and the birds on the card using 3D glue.

Festive cards

No party is complete

without a cake.

What you need
- ❏ *Artoz card: fawn (241), pink (481), pastel blue (413), cornflower blue (425), pastel green (331), algae green (367), honey yellow (243), sunny yellow (247) and bright pink*
- ❏ *Picturel cutting sheet (538)*
- ❏ *ShapeBoss stencil set*
- ❏ *Mini ShapeBoss stencil set*
- ❏ *CardBoss stencil set*
- ❏ *Texture plates*
- ❏ *Candle*
- ❏ *3D glue*

1. Clown
ShapeBoss embossing stencil – Victorian
• Texture plate – Spirit (stars)
Make a pastel green double card (14.8 x 10.5 cm). Cut the front of the card diagonally through the middle as shown in the picture. Cut a fawn rectangle (14.3 x 10 cm). Emboss four patterns from the embossing stencil on the left and right-hand sides of the rectangle and another pattern in the middle. Emboss three patterns along the top and bottom. Draw pencil lines 2 cm from the sides and 3 cm from the top and bottom. Cut the rectangle out of the middle. Stick the frame on an algae green card and cut the algae green card to leave a border. Cut the green rectangle out of the middle. Cut the fawn frame diagonally through the middle, starting in the top left-hand corner and finishing in the bottom right-hand corner. Stick the two halves on the card as shown in the photograph. Make a fawn rectangle (7.5 x 5 cm) and emboss the background on it. Cut the rectangle diagonally through the middle and stick the left-hand half on the algae green card. Cut the algae green card to leave a border and stick the triangle on the front of the card. Stick the right-hand half on an algae green rectangle (7.5 x 5 cm) and emboss the background on the area which is still green. Stick the rectangle on the rear card and stick a picture of a clown on it. Stick the same picture on the front card in exactly the same place. Make the picture 3D.

2. The wedding cake
ShapeBoss embossing stencil – Victorian •
Texture plate – Spirit (hearts)
Make a pink double card (14 x 14 cm). Cut the front of the card diagonally through the middle as shown in the picture. Cut a fawn square (13.4 x 13.4 cm). Emboss three patterns from

1.

2.

3.

4.

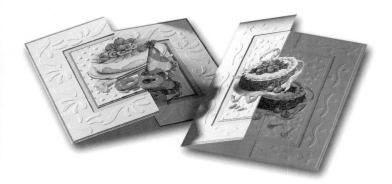

the embossing stencil on all four sides. Draw pencil lines 2 cm from all the edges and cut the square out of the middle. Stick the frame on bright pink card and cut the pink card to leave a border. Cut the bright pink square out of the middle. Cut the fawn frame diagonally through the middle, starting in the top left-hand corner and finishing in the bottom right-hand corner. Stick the two halves on the card as shown in the photograph. Cut a fawn square (8 x 8 cm) and emboss the background on it. Cut the square diagonally through the middle and stick the left-hand half on bright pink card. Cut the bright pink card to leave a border and stick the triangle on the front of the card. Stick the right-hand half on a bright pink square (8 x 8 cm) and emboss the background on the area which is not covered by a picture. Stick the square on the rear card and stick a picture of a wedding cake on it. Stick the same picture on the front card in exactly the same place. Make the picture 3D.

3. The fruit cake
ShapeBoss embossing stencil – Square splash
• *Texture plate – Energy (dots)*
This card is made in the same way as card 2. The front of the card and the small square, however, are cut straight through the middle. The fawn frame is 2.5 cm wide and the square in the middle of the card measures 7.5 x 7.5 cm.

4. The chocolate cake
CardBoss embossing stencil – Congratulations
• *Texture plate – Energy (bubbles)*
This card is made in the same way as card 1. The front and the small rectangle, however, are cut straight through the middle. The fawn frame is 2 cm wide and the rectangle in the middle of the card measures 9.2 x 5.5 cm.

Rose cards

Shiny cards with a

transparent window.

What you need
- ❏ *Canson Mi-Teintes card: almond green (480) and royal blue (495)*
- ❏ *Amaco embossing foil: gold and silver*
- ❏ *Vellum: green and blue*
- ❏ *ShapeBoss stencil set*
- ❏ *Texture plate*
- ❏ *Stylus (small point)*
- ❏ *Contour stickers and matching cutting sheets*
- ❏ *Candle*
- ❏ *3D glue*

Contour stickers
Stick the stickers on the matching contour sheets. Stick the roses on the card using 3D glue.

1. Red rose
ShapeBoss embossing stencil – Square splash • Texture plate – Nature (stone)
Make a blue double card (14 x 14 cm). Draw pencil lines 2.5 cm from the sides on the front of the card and cut the square out of the middle.

Stick blue vellum (14 x 14 cm) on the front of the card. Make a 2.5 cm wide silver frame (13.5 x 13.5 cm) and emboss corner patters and a decorative border on it. Emboss the matching border on the vellum. Cut a silver square (5 x 5 cm) and emboss the background on it.

2. Yellow rose
ShapeBoss embossing stencil – Rectangular wave • Texture plate – Spirit (waves)
Make a blue double card (16 x 12.5 cm). Draw pencil lines 2.5 cm from the sides on the front of the card and cut the rectangle out of the middle. Stick blue vellum (16 x 12.5 cm) on the front of the card. Make a 2.5 cm wide gold frame (15.5 x 12.5 cm) and

emboss corner patters and a decorative border on it. Emboss the matching border on the vellum. Cut a gold rectangle (8 x 4 cm) and emboss the background on it.

3. Two yellow roses

ShapeBoss embossing stencil – Christmas • Texture plate – Spirit (brick)

This card is made in the same way as card 1, except you make a green double card and a gold frame which measures 13.5 x 13.5 cm and is 2 cm wide. The gold square measures 7 x 7 cm.

4. Red rose with a stem

ShapeBoss embossing stencil – Rectangle classic • Texture plate – Spirit (lines)

This card is made in the same way as card 2, except you make a green double card and a silver frame which measures 13.5 x 13.5 cm and is 2.5 cm wide. The silver rectangle measures 7.7 x 4 cm.

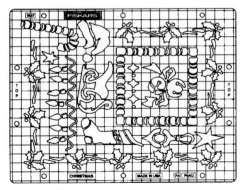

Christmas ShapeBoss stencil

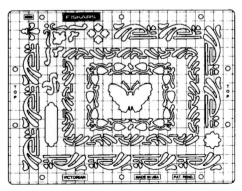

Victorian ShapeBoss stencil

Christmas cards

Use these cards to wish your

family and friends a merry

Christmas.

What you need
- ❏ *Artoz card: red (517) and pastel blue (413),*
  green and ochre
- ❏ *Artoz paper: fawn (241)*
- ❏ *Texture plates*
- ❏ *Stylus: large and small tip*
- ❏ *Marianne Design cutting sheets: 3DA3313*
  and 3DA3314
- ❏ *Border punches*

Punching a continuous border

It is best to use 80-120 gram paper. Place the paper in the punch and push it firmly against the rear of the punch. Squeeze the punch. One complete pattern will be punched. Slide the paper to the left until you can see the white pattern at the end of the punch through the punched out parts of the card. Punch the entire pattern out of the card again. Continue to the end of the strip of paper. To make the pattern continue in the corner, align the side of the paper with the 8th line from the left and squeeze the punch. Continue punching the card as described above. Practice punching the corners with a square piece of scrap paper.

1. Robin redbreast
Texture plate – Energy (dots) • Leaf border punch
Make a green double card (14.8 x 10.5 cm) and stick a red rectangle (14.8 x 9.5 cm) on top. Cut a fawn rectangle (14.8 x 10.5 cm) from paper and punch a continuous border in it. Cut a strip of green card (14.8 x 7 cm) and a strip of red card (14.8 x 2.7 cm). Emboss the background on both strips. The middle of the green strip does not have to be embossed, because the red strip will be placed on top. Stick the layers on the card as shown in the photograph. Decorate the card with a background picture and a robin redbreast on a couple of sprigs of holly. Make the picture 3D using separate pictures from the cutting sheet.

2. Three candles
Texture plate – Energy (squares) • Square border punch
Make a green double card (14.5 x 14.5 cm) and stick an ochre square (13.5 x 13.5 cm) on top.

Cut a fawn square (14.5 x 14.5 cm) from paper and punch a border in it. Cut a pastel blue rectangle (10.5 x 5.2 cm) and emboss the background only on the sides. Cut a green square (8.5 x 8.5 cm) and emboss the background on the area that will not be covered by the picture. Stick the layers on the card as shown in the photograph. Decorate the card with a background picture and candles. Make the picture 3D using separate pictures from the cutting sheet.

3. Birdhouse
Texture plate – Energy (dots) • Heart border punch
Make a red double card (14.5 x 14.5 cm) and stick a green square (13.5 x 13.5 cm) on top. Cut a fawn square (14.5 x 14.5 cm) from paper and punch a border in it. Cut a pastel blue square (10.5 x 10.5 cm) and emboss the background only on the sides. Cut a red square (8.5 x 8.5 cm) and emboss the background on the area that will not be covered by the picture. Stick the layers on the card as shown in the photograph. Decorate the card with a background picture and a birdhouse with some birds. Make the picture 3D using separate pictures from the cutting sheet.

4. Lantern
Texture plate – Spirit (stars) • Holly border punch
Make an ochre double card (14.8 x 10.5 cm). Cut a green rectangle (14.8 x 9.5 cm). Cut a fawn square (14.5 x 14.5 cm) from paper and punch a border in it. Cut two strips: one ochre (14.8 x 7 cm) and one green (14.8 x 2.5 cm). Emboss the background in both strips. The middle of the ochre strip does not have to be embossed, because the green strip will be placed on top. Stick the layers on the card as shown in the photograph. Decorate the card with a background picture and a Christmas scene.
Make the picture 3D using separate pictures from the cutting sheet.

Colourful cards

Every greetings card becomes a present when it has pretty flowers on it.

What you need
- ❏ *Artoz card: fawn (241) and red (517)*
- ❏ *Canson Mi-Teintes card: apple green (475)*
- ❏ *Texture plate*
- ❏ *Stylus: large and small tip*
- ❏ *Marjoleine cutting sheet (pink flowers)*
- ❏ *Marjoleine background sheet/pattern sheet*
- ❏ *Text sticker*
- ❏ *Candle*

Stick all the pictures on green card first and then on the background paper. Cut each layer out so that it is slightly bigger than the previous layer. Stick all the parts together as shown in the photograph.

1. Congratulations
Texture plate – Energy (bubbles)
Make a green double card (14.8 x 10.5 cm) and stick background paper of the same size on top. Cut two strips of card (14 x 5 cm): one from green card and one from fawn card. Emboss the background on both strips. Stick a text sticker on them. Stick all the parts together as shown in the photograph.

2. Window with flowers
Texture plate – Energy (dots)
Make a green double card (14.5 x 14.5 cm) and stick background paper of the same size on top. Cut a green square (14 x 14 cm) and a fawn square (12 x 12 cm). Emboss the background around the sides of both cards. Cut the bottom layer so that it is slightly bigger.

3. Flower corners
Texture plate – Nature (stone)
Make a red double card (14.5 x 14.5 cm). Cut a fawn square (14 x 14 cm) and emboss the background only around the sides. Cut a green square (10 x 10 cm) and emboss the background on it. Stick the square picture on the fawn card first and then on the background paper.

4. Flowers and butterflies
Texture plate – Energy (squares)
Make a red double card (14.8 x 10.5 cm). Cut a strip of fawn card (14.8 x 7 cm) and emboss the background on it. Only emboss the area which will not be covered by the strip. Stick all the parts together as shown in the photograph.

Shiny cards

Shiny cards are suitable for any occasion.

What you need
- ❏ *Artoz card: fawn (241)*
- ❏ *Amaco embossing foil: gold and silver*
- ❏ *Pergamano® vellum: gold and mother-of-pearl*
- ❏ *CardBoss stencil set*
- ❏ *CardBoss stencils (Kars)*
- ❏ *Glitter glue (transparent)*

General information
Use glitter glue to highlight the embossed areas.

Gluing the vellum
Cut the vellum to the correct size. Place it up-side down on a newspaper and spray glue on it. Do this outside! Allow the glue to dry slightly and then stick the vellum on the card. Other types of glue show through the vellum.

1. Baby card
CardBoss embossing stencil – Baby
Make a fawn double card (16 x 12 cm). Cut a rectangle (15.5 x 11.5 cm) from silver embossing foil. Cut a rectangle (15 x 11 cm) from mother-of-pearl vellum and emboss the picture from the stencil on it. Stick the layers on top of each other on the card.

2. Ivy
CardBoss embossing stencil – Ivy
Make a fawn double card (16 x 12 cm). Cut a rectangle (15.5 x 11.5 cm) from mother-of-pearl vellum. Cut a rectangle (15 x 11 cm) from gold embossing foil and emboss the picture from the stencil on it.

3. Stars and bows
CardBoss embossing stencil – Stars and bows
Make a fawn double card (16 x 12 cm). Cut a rectangle (15.5 x 11.5 cm) from mother-of-pearl vellum. Cut a rectangle (15 x 11 cm) from silver embossing foil and emboss the picture from the stencil on it.

4. Christmas trees
CardBoss embossing stencil – Christmas trees
Make a fawn double card (16 x 12 cm). Cut a rectangle (15.5 x 11.5 cm) from gold vellum. Cut a rectangle (15 x 11 cm) from mother-of-pearl vellum and emboss the picture from the stencil on it.

Many thanks to Kars & Co. for supplying the materials.

Shopkeepers can order the materials from Kars & Co B.V. in Ochten, the Netherlands or Vaessen Creative in Nuth, the Netherlands.